Percussive Arts Society International Drum Rudiments

All rudiments should be practiced: open (slow) to close (fast) to open (slow)
and/or at an even moderate march tempo.

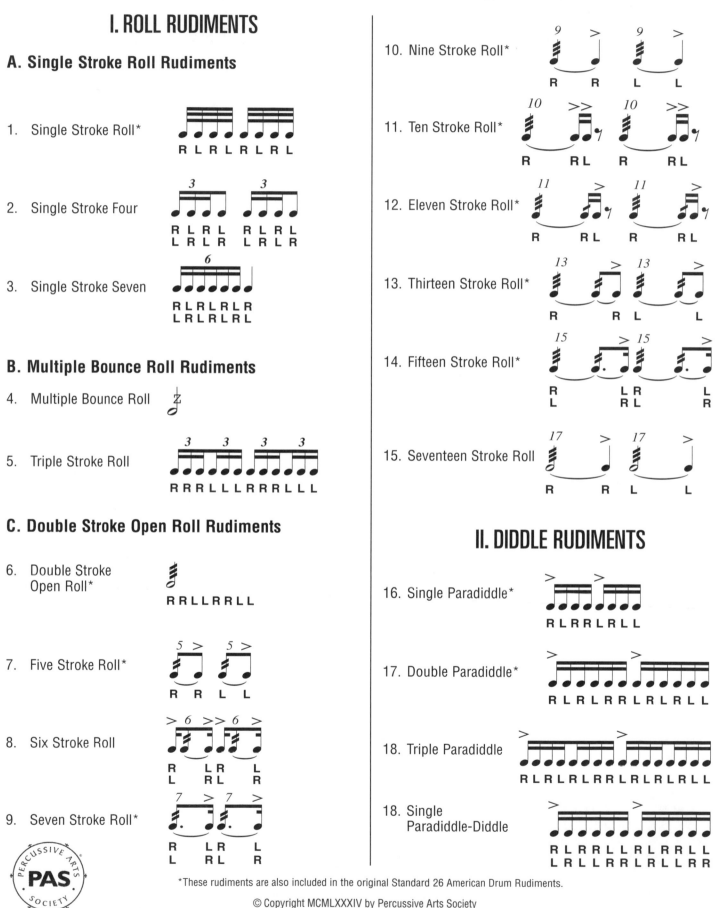

I. ROLL RUDIMENTS

A. Single Stroke Roll Rudiments

1. Single Stroke Roll*
2. Single Stroke Four
3. Single Stroke Seven

B. Multiple Bounce Roll Rudiments

4. Multiple Bounce Roll
5. Triple Stroke Roll

C. Double Stroke Open Roll Rudiments

6. Double Stroke Open Roll*
7. Five Stroke Roll*
8. Six Stroke Roll
9. Seven Stroke Roll*

10. Nine Stroke Roll*
11. Ten Stroke Roll*
12. Eleven Stroke Roll*
13. Thirteen Stroke Roll*
14. Fifteen Stroke Roll*
15. Seventeen Stroke Roll

II. DIDDLE RUDIMENTS

16. Single Paradiddle*
17. Double Paradiddle*
18. Triple Paradiddle
18. Single Paradiddle-Diddle

*These rudiments are also included in the original Standard 26 American Drum Rudiments.

PAS
PERCUSSIVE ARTS SOCIETY
www.pas.org

III. FLAM RUDIMENTS

IV. DRAG RUDIMENTS

For information on becoming a member of the Percussive Arts Society™ contact PAS® at:
701 N.W. Ferris Ave., Lawton, OK 73507 • (580) 353-1456 • E-mail: percarts@pas.org • Web site: www.pas.org

Glossary
Music terms and articulations

Terms

accelerando	Gradually faster
alla marcia	In a march style
a tempo	Return to original tempo or rate of speed
con spirito	Joyfully, and with spirit
crescendo	Gradually louder
decrescendo	Gradually softer
diminuendo (dim.)	Becoming softer
Maestoso	Majestically
molto	Much, very
poco a poco	Little by little
ritardando	Gradually slower
sempre	Always, continually, throughout
simile	Continue in the same manner, style

Tempo Terms

Adagio	A slow movement
Andante	Moderately slow
Andantino	Less moderately, slightly faster than Andante
Allegretto	Moderately fast
Allegro	Quick, lively
Moderato	In moderate time
Prestissimo	Very fast time
Vivace	Lively, brisk, animated

Articulations

>	Accent	Play note with strong attack
Λ	Marcato	Loud emphasized accent
·	Staccato	Short, detached
⌢	Fermata	Hold out
//	Break (Railroad Tracks)	Short pause

Repeat terms and signs

D.C. (Da Capo)	Return to the beginning
D.S. (Dal Segno)	Return to the sign (𝄋)
Fine	End or close
𝄋	Section repeat sign
⊕	Coda sign, ending of an arrangement
D.C. al Fine	Da Capo, return to the beginning, play to fine
D.S. al Fine	Dal Segno, return to the sign (𝄋), play to fine
D.C. al Coda	Da Capo, return to the beginning, play to the coda sign (⊕), and skip to the coda
D.S. al Coda	Dal Segno, return to the sign (𝄋), play to the coda sign (⊕), skip to coda
play 4 times	Repeat as indicated

Dynamics

ppp	Pianississimo	Very, very soft
pp	Pianissimo	Very soft
p	Piano	Soft
mp	Mezzo piano	Moderately soft
mf	Mezzo forte	Moderately loud
f	Forte	Loud
ff	Fortissimo	Very loud
fff	Fortississimo	Very very loud
sfz	Sforzando	Special stress and sudden emphasis
sffz	Sforzatiffimo	Perform with sudden emphasis at a very loud volume
fp	Forte piano	Loud, soft

♩ = Metronome marking

2 ← Measure number

First ending (repeat, take second ending)

Neutral clef (percussion clef)

Bar Line

Music Staff

Repeat sign

Time Signature

Note and Rest Values

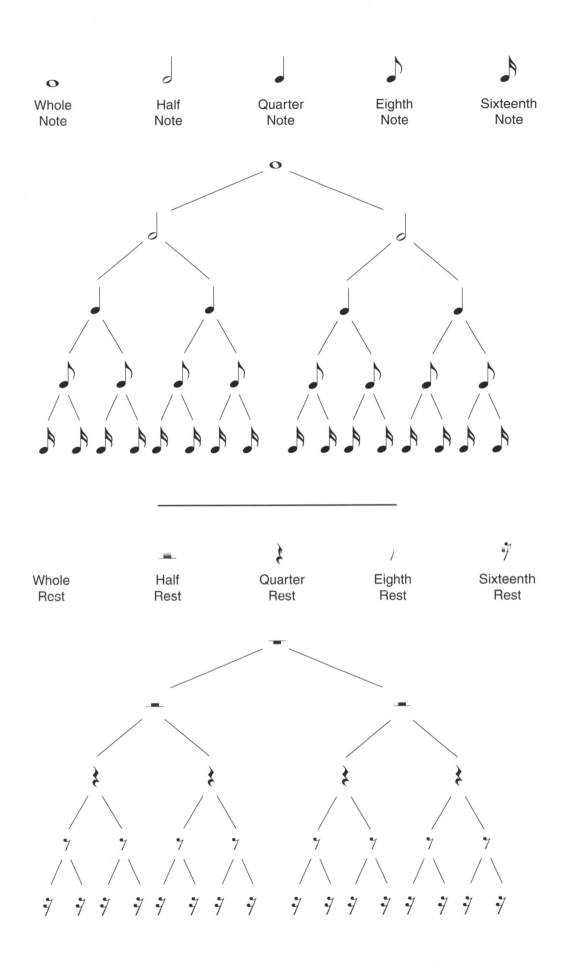

Drum Notation Legend

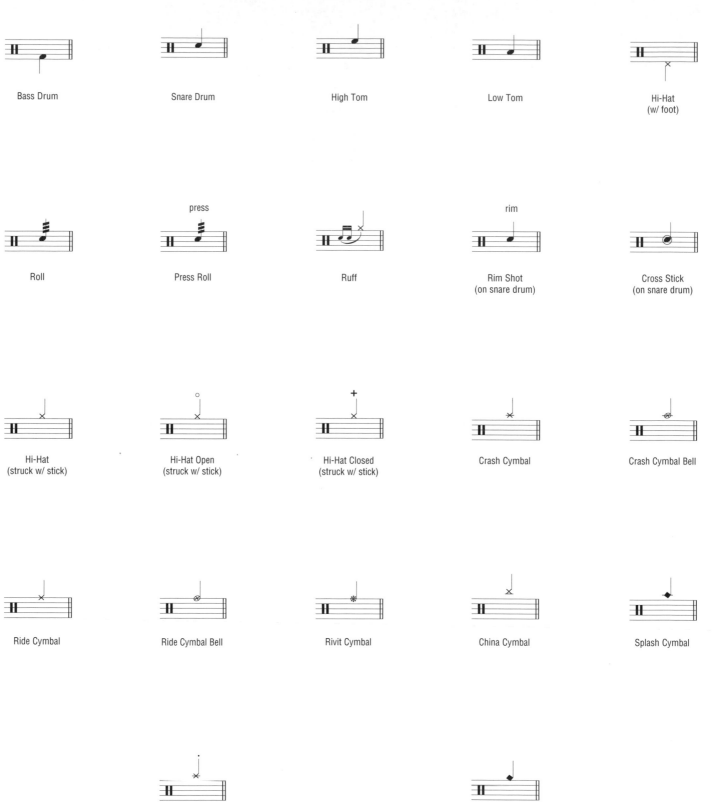